How to Get

PUBLISHED

by K C Murdarasi

GW00375140

TABLE OF CONTENTS

WHO ON EARTH AM I?

And why have I written this book? I'm not a commissioning editor at a top publishing house, I'm not a best-selling household name, I'm just a common-or-garden author with a few titles published and a few more still sitting in a computer folder with electronic dreams of one day being published.

But when I'm at a party, or a wedding, or church, or at any other social occasion where I meet new people, as often as not someone will say to me, "I've got a book/idea for a book. How do I go about getting it published?" This book is my answer.

This is not a foolproof guide to making publishers sit up and take note, and it doesn't guarantee you a six-figure advance. (If you do find out the way to land one of those, please get in touch and let me know.) If you're already in the game of submitting your work and counting your rejection slips, it's probably not going to help you. But if you have a book, an idea for a book, or even just a short story or two, and you'd like to try getting your work published, but you have no idea where to start – this little book is for *you.*

How to Get Published is broken down into non-fiction, novels, and short stories, because the way you go about getting a work published is different in each category. There's also a section on self-publishing, although this book is primarily about getting published by the 'conventional' routes.

Some sections of the book are relevant to more than one type of writing – how to get an agent for non-fiction and for fiction, for example. It's designed so you can go straight to the bits that are relevant to you without having to read the whole thing in order, so feel free to skip over sections.

I've included pointers to helpful resources and useful links, but of course webpages can move and links can break. A bit of quick googling will probably find you something similar to whatever I've mentioned.

There's also a glossary for terms that may be unfamiliar. To look up the meaning of any word in **bold**, go to page 85.

Getting published is hard. I'm not going to pretend otherwise. But the feeling of holding your own work in print is like nothing else. If you're prepared to start the uphill struggle, and you're not afraid of a mixed metaphor, then take a deep breath, and dive in...

NON-FICTION

We'll start with non-fiction because in some ways it's more straightforward, and you can start trying to get your work published before you even finish it, which is nice.

Finding the right publishers

First, go into a bookshop and have a look at some books that are similar to the one you have written, or are writing. I prefer to do this in a real bookshop rather than an online one, because it's easier to browse for the right sort of thing. The books you choose don't have to be exactly the same (in fact you'd hope they aren't, or who's going to buy yours?) but they should be similar in general subject and preferably in tone, too.

Jot down the names of the publishers who released these books. Then go home, or to your local library, and look up the publishers on the internet. (You can also look them up in a recent copy of the Writers and Artists Yearbook, but publishers' websites tend to have a lot more information about how you should submit a book proposal.) Dig around the website until you see a page called something like "information for writers" or "submissions". Sometimes it's on the "Contact Us" page, occasionally the "About

Us". They may say they don't take **unsolicited submissions**, in which case move along and try the next publisher on your list. When you find one that does accept submissions, read their instructions for how you should go about submitting your book or book idea for consideration and then FOLLOW THOSE INSTRUCTIONS TO THE LETTER.

Seriously, there is no quicker way to scupper your chances than by thinking the submission guidelines don't apply to you. If they ask for your first chapter, don't send them your third because you think it's better. If they ask for two chapters, don't send one. Even if they ask for it to be printed on pink tissue paper and delivered by a tame eagle, find a way to comply. Editors receive such a huge bulk of manuscripts that you can't afford to give them an excuse to disregard yours before they even look at it. (By the way, although "manuscript" literally means "written by hand", please don't. If you can't type, find someone who can, and ask/pay/beg them to do it for you.)

Your covering letter

You'll find plenty of guidance online about how to write a killer cover letter, so I'm not going to repeat it here. However, there are some things you should include in your letter (or email, as it normally is):

Who you are

Not just your name, but anything relevant to what you're writing about. If you're writing a book about obesity, mention if you're a dietician, or a Weight Watchers star slimmer, or that you've tried 342 different fad diets.

How to contact you

Yes, if you emailed them they already have your email address, but it's best to put contact details in the manuscript/sample chapter too (unless instructed otherwise by their guidelines), in case it gets orphaned. If you have to submit by post because the regulations demand it, you can still put in a note of your email address.

What the book is like

This isn't just its title and what it's about (although mention those, obviously). How long will the book be? What sort of tone will it take – serious, academic, humorous, chatty? What specific topics will it cover? (Even if you've been asked to include a chapter list, you can still give a couple of stand-out examples in your cover letter.)

Who the book is aimed at

Children? Adults? Teens? Men? Women? People who are interested in history? People from North Devon? Mustachioed bus conductors? Who would buy your book, and why? Don't just assume it's interesting to everyone; it's almost certainly not.

Your connections

Publishers like to know that you'll help them to sell the book. (A writer's work continues long after the book is written, I'm afraid.) Maybe you're a member of a relevant society. Maybe you're not, but you could quickly join one before sending in your application. Maybe you have an impressive social media following, or a blog. Maybe your university has an active alumni network. You get the idea: how many people do you have contact with so that you will eventually be able to try and flog your book to them?

Pictures

Non-fiction books often contain some photographs or other images. Can you supply these? If you can, make that clear when you send your covering letter – but only if they are high quality, not fuzzy holiday snaps.

One last thing – please don't send exactly the same covering letter to each publisher – they have an instinct for that sort of thing. Have a look at their list (that's the books they've published) and let it guide the tone of your letter. You can even mention some books on their list that are similar to yours, to show how your book would be a good fit for that publisher.

But if you must copy and paste, whatever you do, make sure you haven't accidentally left in the name of the other publisher you sent it to! Writing "Dear Publisher B, I would like to submit my book which I feel is a perfect fit for Publisher A" is a recipe for failure.

While you're waiting

You could wait a LONG time for a reply, so you may as well get on with writing the book. If a publisher likes your book proposal they're likely to at least ask for another sample chapter or possibly the whole manuscript. Make sure you have something to send them!

Not-so-secret agents

If you don't get anywhere by pitching your book to publishers, the next step you can try is pitching to agents. There are pros and cons of approaching agents instead of publishers. On the pro side:

- Agents can submit to publishers that don't accept unsolicited submissions. (If it's from a literary agent, that doesn't count as unsolicited – that just applies to us plebs.) That means they have access to the biggest publishers, which have the widest market reach and pay better money.

- Agents have much more experience of the publishing market than you do, and more connections. They know which publisher your book is most likely to be suitable for, and who is on the lookout for particular types of books at the moment.
- If you get a good agent, they can be your friend and champion throughout your literary career.

But on the other hand:

- They take a cut, obviously. This is how they make a living. You are going to give up between 10% and 20% (usually) of your eventual earnings to the agent who got the book placed with a publisher.
- You're not necessarily going to get a good agent. Some may neglect you and let your work fester in a corner while they help other clients, or just take long lunches. There are some agent reviews out there, but not enough to make sure you get someone who is going to give you their utmost effort.
- It's as hard to land an agent as it is a publisher. They're busy too, and inundated with manuscripts. You might get a

rejection, or you might just not hear back. Rejections, both from agents and from publishers, are something you are going to have to get used to if you're serious about getting your book published. I don't think rejections from agents hurt any more than those from publishers, so there's no harm in giving it a try.

When it comes to submitting to an agent, the procedure is pretty much the same as submitting to a publisher, so follow the points above. Again, follow the submission guidelines on the website *to the letter*, or it's your own time you're wasting.

One difference with submitting to agents instead of publishers is that different agents at the same agency may have different interests and specialisms. In some cases you can just submit to a central address, and they will decide who your manuscript is best suited to, but a lot of the time they want you to make that decision – so make it wisely. Have a look at their description of themselves and their interests, and decide if your material fits. Have a look at some of the writers they already represent, and compare your subject area and style to theirs. Be cold and ruthless with yourself when deciding whether you really fit within the subject areas or types of books a particular agent is interested in. If they mostly represent blood-curdling true crime books, your book on amusing true stories of rural police life is *not* close enough.

(Don't tell anyone, but I often e-stalk an editor or agent before I submit, looking at their LinkedIn and Twitter presence to get an idea of what tone they might respond best to – humorous, light and bubbly, po-faced professional etc. I'm not saying it always works, but it doesn't hurt.)

You can, of course, send your manuscript or book proposal to both publishers and agents at the same time. Why not? The publishing industry is unimaginably slow, so if you don't want to die of old age before your book is published, you may as well try as many avenues as possible.

Competitions

One final option to mention is submitting your manuscript to competitions. This will mostly only be relevant if you've finished writing the whole thing. I'm going to talk about competitions in the section on short stories (page 50), so please jump ahead to that section if you can't wait.

NOVELS

Fiction is a different beast. You pretty much have to finish the whole manuscript before you can submit (except in the case of some competitions, which we'll come to), so that's an enormous amount of work before you even start looking for a publisher. If your manuscript is already finished, pat yourself on the back; the proportion of people who would like to write a book someday compared to those who have actually finished one is somewhere around 10,000:1. Okay, I just plucked that figure out of the air, but honestly, there are a lot of people who would like to be in your position.

So now the bad news, if you've already written the book: publishers are usually looking for a particular length of novel, depending on genre. How long? Ask three different people and you'll get three different answers, but the fact is that novels have got longer in recent decades, and where 50,000 words was once considered fairly standard, that's now too short, unless it's young adult fiction. Many publishers are looking for something more like 80,000 – but again, it varies by genre, so use the internet to do some research on the genre of your own novel. (You could start with the Writers & Artists Yearbook website, for example.)

Established writers can publish doorstops or novellas because their publisher already knows that their stuff will sell, but you probably can't. An unknown writer whose book is 'too long' or 'too short' faces an extra barrier to publication, and it's hard enough already, so when you start submitting, try to make sure it's at least close to the typical length for the genre.

By the way, when I say 'doorstop' I mean lo-o-ong novels (the breeze-block size that are big enough to hold a door open with, you see) and novellas are 'little novels' – anything from about 20,000 to 40,000 words, depending on how you define it.

A quick note here: we *always* talk about the length of a manuscript in words, not in pages. Your "100-page novel" could be 300,000 words of closely-spaced, tiny print, or about 10,000 of double-spaced Arial 16-point. Talking about your book's length in pages (before it's published) just marks you out as an amateur – which you are, at this stage, but there's no need to let it show.

Finding the right publishers

As with non-fiction, you have to start by finding a publisher who actually publishes your kind of book. Yes, the big publishers like Penguin will publish every genre there is, but you're not submitting your work to Penguin, because, surprise surprise, they don't accept unsolicited submissions. You would need an agent for that – which is in the next section.

When you're targeting smaller publishers, where you have a better chance, it's likely they will specialise in certain genres, and there is no point in sending them your manuscript if it's not the kind of thing they publish.

There are two main ways to find a suitable publisher:

1) Go to a bookshop and look at books that are in the same genre. Be a little more specific than just "romance" or "science fiction", though – those are *broad* categories. Is it the same temperature of romance? The same hardness of sci-fi? Probably many of the books you find will be by the "big five" publishers, who don't take unsolicited submissions (Hachette, HarperCollins,

Macmillan, Penguin Random House, and Simon & Schuster). Ignore those, and make a note of the names of the other ones.

or

2) Trawl through the list of publishers in a recent edition of the Writers & Artists Yearbook, reading the descriptions of what genres they accept, and whether they accept unsolicited submissions. Write down a list of ones you will try, or if it's your own copy, pencil in a star by the name of the agent.

Then hop on the internet to check the publishers' websites. Score off all the ones that don't accept **unsolicited submissions** (also sometimes called "unagented submissions") or rub out the pencil star. Then read the submission guidelines of the ones that do, VERY CAREFULLY. And then follow them. Punctiliously.

A warning: If you simply type "publishers" or "publish my book" or similar things into the search box, myriad links will appear from publishers who are apparently desperate to consider your book for publication. Don't click on them. These are what are called **vanity publishers**. They are often unscrupulous and mainly want to part you from your money. Real publishers don't have to advertise for manuscripts; they're drowning in them.

That's not to say that all self-publishing (where you pay to have your book published) is dodgy. I'll talk a bit more about that at the end of the book. But generally speaking, if a publisher is keen to see your book without knowing anything about it or you – run away.

Your synopsis

Publishers are likely to ask for a sample of the book – the first two chapters, the first

5,000 words, something like that – which varies from publisher to publisher. They'll also want you to send a **synopsis**.

I can't speak for any other writers, but the thought of writing synopses makes my heart sink. However, like many of life's unpleasant tasks, it has to be done.

A synopsis sums up the whole plot of your book in a few paragraphs. It is not the same as a blurb; it's not a tease to get people to read it, it's a full, albeit very short, description to help a publisher decide whether to take it on. To be absolutely clear: yes, you do give away that killer twist you saved for the final chapter. No, you don't tell give them a blow-by-blow account of what happens in every single chapter.

(Sometimes publishers will ask for a chapter list. This is different from a synopsis because in a chapter list you really do give them a couple of sentences about what happens in every single chapter. But if the submission instructions just say 'synopsis', they're not looking for that level of detail.)

Writing a good synopsis is hard. You'll probably get better with practice, but for now just grit your teeth and write the best potted description of your book that you can, including things like

- **Genre**
- Setting
- Main characters
- Basic plot (including spoilers)

Sometimes publishers may want an '**elevator pitch**' too, and even if they don't, it can be a good exercise just so you can quickly express what your book is really like. If you had to describe your book in a couple of sentences, or one tweet, what would you say?

Here are some examples from my own books:

An illuminating, informative and really quite sarcastic trawl through what we actually know about one of England's most famous heroes.

(*Why Everything You Know about Robin Hood Is Wrong* – non-fiction)

Kidnapped as a young boy and sold into slavery, Patrick learnt to forgive the unforgiveable. His sacrifice would leave a legacy of faith that would last through the centuries.

(*Patrick of Ireland: The Boy Who Forgave* – novelised biography)

Leda is facing forced marriage. Suela is facing slavery. Their country is descending into chaos. To stand any chance of escape they must rely on each other, their wits, and God.

(*Leda* – novel)

If you're really struggling with your synopsis or elevator pitch, you could always ask a friend to read it and give you their take. A bit of distance can help. But only ask friends who seem genuinely keen to read your

SHORT STORIES

I own a wonderful old book, currently out of print, called *Short Stories: How to Write Them* by Cecil Hunt. It is very helpful if you want to improve your short story writing, and I would heartily recommend getting hold of a copy if you can. But while I love Hunt's practical advice and reading recommendations, the book does make me sigh with longing for an earlier time, the time Hunt was writing, when most major newspapers and innumerable magazines published general-interest short fiction. That time has long since passed away.

47

So where can you get short stories published today? There are still a few outlets, but they tend to be for specific genres. There are quite a few magazines that still publish 'women's' stories – warm and cosy stories, or romance, or warm and cosy romance. (Try *People's Friend*, *Woman's Weekly* or *Take a Break*.) And then there are some magazines, mostly online and mostly in the USA, that publish science fiction stories (you can find a list here: https://www.writersincharge.com/fantasy-sci-fi-magazines-that-pay/). And there are also magazines, often run by or out of universities, that publish 'literary' short stories (e.g. The Ogilvie, Bone and Ink Press,

Craft). But if your stories aren't cosy/romance, sci fi or high literature, you may struggle to find a traditional market.

As for trying to get a collection of short stories published as a book, forget it. You have to already be famous or established as a writer in order to get a collection of short stories published. If you can't find a magazine that suits your work, what's left to you is **anthologies**. And how do you get your story into an anthology? Usually by winning a competition.

Competition time

Hello and welcome if you have just joined us from the non-fiction or novel sections! The pros and cons of entering writing competitions are as follows:

Pro:

- Someone will definitely read your work. The same can't be said for submissions to publishers.
- You could win stuff! Usually it's money, but sometimes it's a writing course or other prize. (I once came first in a travel writing competition where the top prize was a spiritual retreat, and I

was gutted because the second prize was a year's supply of ice cream!)

- It often leads to publication. Even if publication isn't part of the prize itself, you will usually be put in touch with publishers or agents who may be interested.

Con:

- They cost money, and the longer the piece of work, the higher the fee. Short story competitions are often free, or under a fiver, but novel competitions can be £25+, and that adds up, especially if you're a starving artist. (It's less of a concern if writing is secondary to your day job as a hedge-fund manager.)

- The cheaper the contest, the more people enter it – obviously – so you've got more competition. Also, the cheaper the competition, the less prestigious, and the less likely to offer a monetary prize as well as publication. That's not a major concern, at least when you're starting out, but you don't want to end up with your work published among such a bag of dross that you're embarrassed to even tell people about it. And it can happen. (Although obviously I'm not naming any names – because I'm embarrassed to tell people about it.)

- Entering them takes time, and organization. Hands up who loves admin? Thought not.

So if you do decide you'd like to enter a writing contest, how do you go about it?

First of all, you have to find a competition. You can just do a web search, especially for lists of short story (or novel, or non-fiction) competitions, and you'll probably turn up some useful results. Alternatively, you can buy a magazine such as *Writing*, which has a Writer's News section at the back, full of competitions and potential markets for your work. In April they usually have a pull-out section with a list of competitions for the whole year. That's worth the four or five quid it will cost you. You can also sign up for emails from *OnthePremises.com*, who have regular short story competitions and advice for aspiring writers.

Next, you have to enter your work. I've said it before but I'm going to say it again: *follow the instructions*. If you've got the details of the competition from *Writing* magazine or some third-party website, check the website of the actual competition to make sure you're doing it right. They may specify:

- Word count
- **Genre**
- Theme
- Line spacing (double, single or 1.5)
- Font (you're usually safe with Times New Roman 12-point, but check!)
- File type (usually .doc is fine, but some insist on .rtf)
- Whether your details should appear in your submission file
- How you pay (usually PayPal, sometimes direct to the website)

Whatever they ask for, you either do it, or you don't bother entering, because there is absolutely no point in entering a competition and not following the rules. Your entry will most likely be discarded unread, and you will have lost your entry fee plus your time and effort.

If you're on Twitter, you should also look out for the occasional 'tweet pitch' competitions, where you tweet your **elevator pitch** using a specific hashtag. Publishers scan the tweets for anything that grabs them, and may invite you to send more information if you've piqued their interest.

If you're not on Twitter, you probably should be; it's the most important social media network for writers, and very handy for networking. Sometimes finding opportunities to get published is a case of "who you know, not what you know", so having a network of other people in the writing business can be handy. The nice thing about Twitter, given how much most writers enjoy networking (we tend to be introverts), is that you can do this without actually having to talk to people.

For another method of networking, see the section on beta readers (page 81).

Good old admin

Ah yes, that admin I mentioned earlier. You were hoping I'd forgotten about it, weren't you? But unfortunately, if you're going to take this submitting business seriously, you will need to keep track of what you've submitted, where, and when. This is especially true for magazines and competitions that don't accept **simultaneous submissions**, because you need to know whether the story you're planning to submit is already 'out' or not.

Cecil Hunt, in *Short Stories: How to Write Them*, recommends using index cards, one for each story, and recording the submission information on them. That may still work for you if you like a physical filing system, but these days it's probably easier to do it electronically, using a spreadsheet or a database.

Personally, I use a spreadsheet, with a row for each story, columns for where it's been submitted, and colour coding to indicate whether it's been published or not. I could describe this at great length to allow you to replicate it, but it seems kinder just to let you download a version of it that you can use yourself. Type the following link into your internet browser: http://tiny.cc/8re5az

What about afterwards?

When you enter a short story competition, they usually give you some indication of when the winning entries will be decided. You may or may not be informed directly if you've lost (don't worry, you will be if you've won), but you can go back to the website after the appointed date and have a look at the list of winners. Then you can cross it off your list (or rather, record the result in your spreadsheet) and move on to another competition.

Magazines may or may not ever get back to you. You'll just have to decide for yourself when you want to give up and write it off. This is one reason why we put a date in the spreadsheet, so you can see when it's been six months or a year with no response. Even if a magazine or competition doesn't accept simultaneous submissions, they can't expect you to wait forever to hear back from another market, or you wouldn't have any stories left, so just consider it rejected when you think a reasonable amount of time has passed. Honestly, you wouldn't believe the number of times "no answer" is recorded in my own submissions spreadsheet.

And what about if you do *quite* well? Say you're longlisted, shortlisted or you get an

honourable mention, but you're not actually published? Psychologically, you use that as a means to stop yourself falling into a pit of despair and deciding you will never write again. Practically, it can be useful in showing that you're a decent writer, which improves your chances of getting published in the future. Publishers are more likely to give the time of day to a novel or non-fiction piece that has been shortlisted for a prize (or even won). Or if you choose to self-publish a collection of short stories, for instance, it gives the potential reader confidence if at least one of the stories has already been judged to be pretty good.

And if you do win, and your story or novel is published? Congratulations! You no longer need my advice – but if you become rich and famous, do remember to give me a plug.

WHAT ABOUT SELF-PUBLISHING?

If getting published by conventional means just isn't working for you, or you simply don't want to wait that long, you could always self-publish. As with everything else, there are pros and cons.

Pro:

- It's comparatively quick compared to conventional publishing, which can be measured in ice ages.
- You get to keep all of your profits, not just a **royalty.**

- You can publish work that doesn't fit into a conventional genre or typical word count.
- You have more control. (Conventional publishers may change the title, choose the cover art etc., and not give you much say.)
- If your book gets good reviews or generates good sales, that's a reason for a traditional publisher to consider your next book.

Con:

- There's a stigma attached. Your book may be just as good as one that's conventionally published, or you might be self-publishing it because it's a pile of pants that no decent publisher would sully their hands on. There's no way to tell without reading it. Therefore, you will have a very hard time persuading a bookshop to stock it.

- It's easy to be duped by unscrupulous self-publishing services (**vanity publishers**) with hidden fees, terrible service or unfair terms and conditions.
- It's hard to find an audience for your book. It's a crowded market out there, and you probably don't have Penguin's advertising budget.
- It usually costs money:

- Typesetting
- Proofreading (You may think you can skip this one. Don't.)
- Admin (Registration in online catalogues, copies for national libraries etc.)
- Cover design (Don't try this at home unless you're *very* good.)

- Even if you do all the legwork, or call in favours, you've still got to meet the production costs, which are higher for small print runs. (This doesn't apply to ebook-only publication, of course.)
- You have to deal with all the legal headaches. Do you know how many copies you're required to send to the

British Library (if you're in the UK), or what the rules are about quoting song lyrics? No? Then better swot up.

There are companies that can help with a lot of the tricky stuff, which are often self-publishing arms of conventional publishers (e.g. Matador, which is a self-publishing imprint of the publisher Troubador), but what you save in brain-ache, you pay for in cash. Publishing services don't come cheap.

I'm not trying to put you off self-publishing, but please understand that it's not as easy as it's sometimes made out to be, and it's not a get-rich-quick scheme – but then, neither is being conventionally published.

Here are some of the better-known self-publishing platforms:

Kindle Direct Publishing (KDP) from Amazon. Good for ebooks, with certain incentives if you make your book available only through them. Pretty rubbish for print books; you may throw your computer through the wall after you try to upload your cover page in the correct dimensions for the fortieth time. But it is free.

<u>Lulu</u>. I haven't used it, but I have been published in anthologies that have used this platform. It's been around for a while, is well-regarded, and does ebooks and print. Prices start from free.

<u>Smashwords</u>. Ebook only. Free, but a bit tricky to use, so you might need to pay someone to format your book correctly before it can be uploaded. They have good promotions every year, but their online platform is rickety. I often get an error message when I try to access it, even from different browsers.

Matador. Not cheap, but very professional, and they are pretty upfront about fees and services. Kind of slow, though. They also do distribution, using the same channels as for their conventionally-published books, which is important if you want your book to be available in normal bookshops.

IngramSpark – Ingram is a big name in book distribution, and IngramSpark is its self-publishing arm. There's an upfront cost, even for ebooks (do a bit of googling to see if you can find a promo code, or wait for a special offer), but the quality is high and, obviously, distribution is included, since that's their thing. A good, low-cost route to get your book into the catalogues that real bookshops and libraries order from.

If you decide to go ahead with self-publishing, there are lots of books and websites (e.g. BookBaby.com) that can help. Try your local library. Or if you would like me to produce an expanded guide to self-publishing, please get in touch through my website (kcmurdarasi.com) to let me know.

ENDWORD

That's the end of this little book/glorified pamphlet on how to go about getting published, save for the glossary and FAQs. I hope you have found it helpful. I haven't sugar-coated things, because you'll have to be pretty strong if you're going to go down this road – or at least have strong drink to hand. But if you long to see your name in print, and to read Amazon reviews by real people saying they enjoyed your book, then welcome to the club!

To balance out all the cynicism, sarcasm and dire warnings, I'm going to leave you with an inspirational poem by Edward Guest. He absolutely churned out poetry in the early part of the twentieth century, much of it sentimental drivel, but some of it better than that. This is his best, in my opinion, and justifies his whole oeuvre:

It Couldn't Be Done

Somebody said that it couldn't be done

But he with a chuckle replied

That "maybe it couldn't," but he would be one

Who wouldn't say so till he'd tried.

So he buckled right in with the trace of a grin

On his face. If he worried he hid it.

He started to sing as he tackled the thing

That couldn't be done, and he did it!

Somebody scoffed: "Oh, you'll never do that;

At least no one ever has done it;"

But he took off his coat and he took off his
hat

And the first thing we knew he'd begun it.

With a lift of his chin and a bit of a grin,

Without any doubting or quiddit,

He started to sing as he tackled the thing

That couldn't be done, and he did it.

There are thousands to tell you it cannot be
done,

There are thousands to prophesy failure,

There are thousands to point out to you one by one,
The dangers that wait to assail you.
But just buckle in with a bit of a grin,
Just take off your coat and go to it;
Just start in to sing as you tackle the thing
That "cannot be done," and you'll do it.

FREQUENTLY ASKED QUESTIONS

Q. Who should look over the work before I submit it to publishers/agents?

A. It is always a good idea to get some feedback. There are three kinds of feedback you can get:

1. Proofreading. This means correcting the errors in your writing – spelling, grammar, punctuation, sentence formation etc.

   You can easily find a professional proofreader online (e.g. on

PeoplePerHour.com), but anyone with excellent grammar and spelling, and some free time, can do this for you. Unless this person is a very close relative, you should either pay them or give them a nice gift.

2. Editing (there are different kinds of editing, but let's not get into that here). This is about improving weaknesses in the book itself – problems with the structure, things that don't make sense, overused words or phrases. It's not just about typos.

This should be done by a professional, or at least someone who is active in the literary field, such as another author. Again, you should pay them/reward them in some way – editing is not the same as reading a book for fun.

3. Beta readers. These people don't have to be professionals, just people you know (friends, colleagues, social media contacts) who like to read, and who are prepared to give you comments. You might want to buy these people a coffee, or mention them in your acknowledgements, but you wouldn't

normally pay them because, hopefully, they already want to read your book.

They are not professionals, and they will give you a reader's opinion on what the book is like, which were the best and worst bits, and whether they thought it worked altogether. A note: you can ask your mum to be a beta-reader if you like, but please take her opinion with a tablespoon of salt. She's your mum – of course she thinks it's all great.

Q. Is it OK to send my book to multiple publishers at once? What if one says yes? Can you cancel the other submissions?

A. I would say it's fine to send **simultaneous submissions** for novels and non-fiction books. Publishers are often unimaginably slow in responding, and sometimes don't respond at all. Their failure to respond doesn't mean you can never send your book proposal to anyone else! If you do get a firm offer from one publisher, just send a quick, polite line to any publishers who haven't replied yet, telling them it's no longer available. (This is where keeping a spreadsheet is helpful again.)

The only time this would be a problem is in competitions and magazines, which have shorter turnaround times. In these cases, if they say they don't accept simultaneous submissions, just don't do it. Or do it, and face the tiny risk of some embarrassment if your book or story is selected/awarded a prize by more than one. Up to you.

GLOSSARY

Anthology
A collection of works by different authors. Literally "a garland of flowers", if you're into your etymology.

Elevator pitch
A sentence or two that sums up what your book is about and makes it sound appealing.

Genre
The category a piece of writing falls into, for example thriller, romance, black comedy.

Honourable mention	A virtual pat on the back, when you don't get placed in a competition, but the judge(s) think your entry is good enough to be commended.
Royalty	A percentage of a book's sale profits paid to you by your publisher.
Simultaneous submissions	Sending the same piece to more than one competition or potential market at the same time.
Synopsis	A brief but complete description of the book's contents.

Typesetting	Preparing the book for publishing by arranging the text as it will look on the page – layout, font, page numbering etc.
Unsolicited submissions	Sending your work directly to a publisher, rather than your agent sending it for you.
Vanity publishers	Companies that charge authors high prices for self-publishing, often providing a bad service. They may masquerade as traditional publishers who just need you to pay a 'contribution' towards their costs.

ACKNOWLEDGEMENTS

I would like to thank my friend and editor Dayspring Jubilee MacLeod for her helpful corrections, suggestions and words of encouragement, and Amy Kingham for giving me feedback from an aspiring author's point of view. And through gritted teeth I also thank all the strangers who have cornered me at parties and quizzed me about how to get published. Although I realise that doctors have it worse.

Printed in Great Britain
by Amazon

15215080R00052